ically, investors end up paying more for the fund than it is worth.

The
INVESTOR'S
SURVIVAL GUIDE

The INVESTOR'S SURVIVAL GUIDE

Basic Training for All Investors With additional chapter on
"HOW TO GET OUT OF DEBT"

Joseph A. Castelluccio, Jr.

authorHOUSE®

AuthorHouse™ LLC
1663 Liberty Drive
Bloomington, IN 47403
www.authorhouse.com
Phone: 1-800-839-8640

© 2014 Joseph A.Castelluccio, Jr.. All rights reserved.

No part of this book may be reproduced, stored in a retrieval system, or transmitted by any means without the written permission of the author.

Published by AuthorHouse   06/04/2014

ISBN: 978-1-4969-1194-0 (sc)
ISBN: 978-1-4969-1193-3 (hc)
ISBN: 978-1-4969-1184-1 (e)

Library of Congress Control Number: 2014908824

Any people depicted in stock imagery provided by Thinkstock are models, and such images are being used for illustrative purposes only. Certain stock imagery © Thinkstock.

This book is printed on acid-free paper.

Because of the dynamic nature of the Internet, any web addresses or links contained in this book may have changed since publication and may no longer be valid. The views expressed in this work are solely those of the author and do not necessarily reflect the views of the publisher, and the publisher hereby disclaims any responsibility for them.

TABLE OF CONTENTS

Introduction ix
Chapter 1 You Have the Skills, Use Them 1
Chapter 2 Don't Fall Victim to the "Sugar Rush" 9
Chapter 3 Get on the Bondwagon 17
Chapter 4 Choosing Stocks: As Easy as 1, 2, 3 25
Chapter 5 Balance Risk 33
Chapter 6 Certificates of Deposit a.k.a CDs 41
Chapter 7 How Much Should
           My Initial Investment Be? 45
Chapter 8 Kids Can Have Fun Investing, Too 53
Chapter 9 The Generic Person 59
Chapter 10 How To Get Out Of Debt 63
Summary 73
Glossary 75

I want to dedicate this book to my wife of 45 years and my two wonderful, loving children. I believe a man's wealth is measured by his family, That said, my wife, my son, and my daughter have made me the richest man in the world.

Introduction

Values—we look for them every day. Whether we're buying food, clothing, cars, or other essentials, comparison shopping plays a vital role in our daily purchases. Even if we don't do it consciously, we are all bargain hunters at heart. Yet despite this basic training learned in the supermarkets and department stores, we often ignore our instincts when it comes to making investment decisions. We instead place our hard-earned money in low-yielding investments or lock ourselves into situations that in effect limit our ability to increase our net worth. This dilemma has a solution, and that's what this book is all about. I'm going to share with you the best-kept secret. It's an investment vehicle that I'm sure all of you have heard of. However, I'm equally certain that if you do own any it's such a small amount that you're terribly underweighted. Quite frankly, this tool is not supposed to be a secret at all; it just seems to have turned out that way. Before I tell you what this tool is, I want to welcome you and thank you for the opportunity to let me share my secret weapon with you. They say the best place to hide something is right in front of you, because that is the last place anyone will look. Well, that's exactly what we have here. I will give you a hint—my secret is the largest marketplace in the world.

I would like to begin by saying that I am very pleased and flattered that you chose to read my book. You undoubtedly have certain expectations and goals that you hope this book will fulfill. Therefore, I want you to know that I am totally committed, dedicated, and obligated to fill all of your expectations. I am also confident that I will. I'll even go one step further and say that I think you will find upon completing the book that it was everything that you thought it would be and much more.

Next, it's important to mention that I want to put myself in your place and try to answer the one question that would be the most obvious. Why is this book different from all the other ones that are out there? When people ask good questions, they deserve good answers.

The short answer is that this book will empower you to go out and take charge of your financial destiny. However, I want to go a little further and give you several reasons why I believe this book will separate itself from the rest of the pack. Then I will build on those points as we go along.

I want you to know what this book does try to do and what it definitely does not try to do. I offer no apologies up front for the uncomplicated solutions to everyday financial problems. Some people think that if something is not complicated, it's not sophisticated; therefore, it won't work. An old saying sums it up best: Keep it simple, silly (KISS). My solutions will be easy to understand, and the time frame for results will provide a gradual, steady progression toward your goals. The results will be sophisticated; the approach will be simple to undertake. That's why it's so important for you to be involved in the process. Who knows your goals and when there's a change in your life better than you do? We're all at different stages in our lives and careers; therefore, the plans will vary, and the stages will always be changing.

Be patient and keep reminding yourself that investing is a journey in which direction is much more important than speed. Also keep in mind that you are getting this information from someone who has been involved in the investment industry for more than 35 years. I have been actively involved in all the markets on a daily basis—giving advice, trading, selling, marketing, investing, and most important, listening.

Yes, that's correct, I said listening. Listening is the key. I've been in the company of countless clients and professionals. I've traveled to scores of cities, large and small. Remarkably, the message I hear everywhere is the same, and it is plain and simple. *I want to maximize my return and preserve my principal.* I plan to show you how to do that and more. So, if I may borrow a comment from the distinguished laureate Albert Einstein, "Make everything as simple as possible, but not simpler."

One thing this book won't do is teach you to predict the swings in the markets. No one can know how all markets will move all the time. Intelligent investment advisers realize that their value doesn't lie in predicting market timing. Instead, they earn their keep by simply helping investors reach their financial goals.

Another thing I'm not going to do is try to compare the performance of one security to that of another security in an attempt to discredit one or the other. No panacea product exists. If it did, everybody would be buying it. Instead, *diversification* is critical. More specifically, it's the main ingredient everyone needs. Diversification is absolutely essential in attaining the balance you need if you expect your investments to succeed.

Why is it that we accept the concept of a balanced diet when we sit down to eat but ignore a "balanced diet" when we sit down to invest? Diversification and balance are helpful in all aspects of life, but they are requirements for investing. In this book, I'll show you the balance you need. I don't want you to change your mind about how you invest; on the contrary, I want to encourage you to use your mind. This book will dispel old myths, particularly the ones that claim the markets are meant for institutions only. The markets belong to all investors, big and small. The problem arises when investors think the markets are casinos. Markets are for investing; casinos are for gambling. Finally, I will encourage you to save more and instill confidence in your ability to accomplish that goal. The more involved you get, the greater your confidence will grow. That confidence will feed on itself, and your participation will increase, as well.

Chapter 1

You Have the Skills, Use Them

Think back to the subtitle of this book: *Basic Training for All Investors*. What is the intention of basic training in the military? Basic training is designed to give you the knowledge and to fine-tune the instincts that will prepare you for combat with an unknown foe. In the military, these skills will help *save your life*. Similarly, the intention of getting the proper basic training as an investor is to give you the knowledge and to fine-tune the instincts that will prepare you for combat with an unknown marketplace. As an investor, these skills will help *save your money*.

The purpose of this book is not to rewrite economic theories or to give historic background. Aside from possibly being academically stimulating, such publications frequently leave the readers more confused than ever about investing. It would be intellectually dishonest to assume that after you read those texts you will be any more able to invest your money than before you read them. Why? Simply because they assume that you understand the language of the markets.

To clarify this idea, if I read a book in a foreign language, would I understand what the book is about? Of course not! I would need to have someone interpret it. The world of investing has its own type of language, so if you read a book that doesn't interpret the terminology and show you how to use it, much if not all of the information is lost in the translation.

Let me give you an example. Recently, several so-called market timers, meaning the people who claim to know the right time to buy and sell, were explaining the current overall economic situation and attempting to give guidance and shed wisdom to those who were assembled. It went something like this. The conventional wisdom is that the market will rally when the war begins. Given that, the smart money will bet that the consensus has already been discounted in the market, so the contrary is more likely to occur. Therefore, stock prices will more likely decline, not rally. However, as everyone knows, the consensus is always wrong, so we could see a rally anyway. Does that clarify the situation for you? I don't know how much you got out of that, but my brain hurts each time I read things like that. Don't give me timing, give me time.

Knowledge is great; however, knowing how to use it is another thing entirely. Some teachers are bright and extremely knowledgeable, but they don't know how to convey the message clearly. Many other publications focus on what I call "glossary knowledge." They provide definitions, historical information, charts, and ratios. All that data does is show you the past. It does not tell you what will happen in the future. This is the information age and we're on the information highway. The trick is to get the information you need and want on the information highway while avoiding becoming roadkill along the way.

Getting too much data can be as bad as not getting enough. The difference between enough and not enough is simple. Can you make a decision on the data you just received, or was too much extraneous information included?

Think about your local weather report as one example. You get the barometric pressure, several satellite shots of the weather patterns, Fahrenheit and Celsius temperatures, as well as information about low-pressure and high-pressure systems in the area. You also get all that same information for the entire country. And then, of course, who could go to bed without knowing the historic temperatures and precipitation for that date. Although all of that information might be interesting to some, all you really need to know is the temperature and whether it is going to rain or snow. When you get dressed in the morning you just want to know how to dress for today's weather. When investing, most people want to know what, where, when, and most important how to invest. Instead, they get a lot of information that in most cases belongs only in the "nice-to-know" category. When you ask someone for the time, you don't want to hear how to build a watch. In this book, I simply give you what you need—the time.

Most people read various publications and books and come away feeling "financially challenged." Many of these individuals have college degrees and think they should understand what to do. Instead, they become so intimidated and overwhelmed that they become frustrated, hence they seek outside help. This doesn't mean that if you read a book on brain surgery and feel equally frustrated and confused that you should still attempt to try the at-home method in your living room. No pun intended. You don't have to be a brain surgeon to understand my method of investing.

If you think that reading those other texts can teach you what you need to know, try buying an unassembled swing set. Then attempt to assemble it just by reading the directions (no pictures). Even those of you who are successful will admit that perhaps this positive result was a one-time event. The knowledge one gained from that exercise could easily be the knowledge that you should never try such an exercise again.

In addition, financial books typically have disclaimers indicating that the information might not be accurate and that past performance doesn't guarantee future results. With such a disclaimer, why did the author bother writing it and why did you bother reading it in the first place? This could be the reason why so many people seek so-called professional advice.

Just use some common sense and this book will do the rest. What I want to do is take the average person, professional, brain surgeon, rocket scientist, or even the so-called seasoned investor and show them the commonsense approach to successful investing. I'll show you how to take your everyday innate skills of *prudence, intellect,* and *perceptiveness* and apply them so you can understand how to reach your financial goals.

These are the same skills that you use each day whether you are shopping for clothing or food, and the same skills that you use when you are preparing to take a trip. It is not an exaggeration to say that some people spend more time shopping for a pen than they do shopping for the right investment. I want to give you the right mindset to break things down to their basic common denominator so you can feel as comfortable investing as you do shopping for your favorite item.

It often amazes me how most people will put enormous preparation into a shopping extravaganza at a mall, or some mundane food shopping at the supermarket. The detail that they put into it is incredible and often can be amusing.

Let's illustrate a couple of typical shopping outings and see if you can identify with some or all of the examples. Let's begin with a trip to the mall. What outfit should you wear? After all you have to have the right look or you won't look like you belong there. You know what I mean, right! My mom always said, "If you want to get where you want to be, you have to look like you're already there." Next, what are the mall hours? Time is critical . . . especially if try-ons are required.

Time is also needed for browsing. Browsing gives shoppers the opportunity to "save" money. During browse time, shoppers decide to buy things they didn't come for but couldn't pass up because they were on sale; hence, they save money by spending more on the things that cost less. Does this sound familiar?

The next phrase is borrowed from the real estate industry: "location, location, and location." Shoppers take location seriously, too. What mall has the right stores for the merchandise they seek? Which store should they go to first and what sequence should they then follow? What level do they want to begin on, and where do they want to finish? The last store location should be coordinated with the closing of the mall and the proper exit door so shoppers can end up where their car is located. As you can see, mall shopping requires a great deal of strategic planning.

Next, let's consider the food shoppers. They have a different approach, but the basic concept is the same. Food shoppers come armed with sale bulletins and coupons that were clipped and sorted in anticipation of the trip. They know that certain weekdays bring special bargains.

Next of course is location . . . to food shoppers, location also is critical as they first plan the right aisle to start the assault.

Will you need one cart or two—that of course depends on how many bulky items you are getting. Next, give some thought to the weight and size of the items you are planning to acquire, heavy items of course first, lighter ones on top. A slip-up here and your white bread looks deformed. It's no fun trying to put mutilated white bread into those perfect slots in the toaster.

Then, as you move up and down the aisles you must remember not to forget to separate the food items from the detergents. It's a rude awakening when you forgot to do that and the next morning you find that your cereal tastes like lemon bleach. Now the most critical part of your mission, leave the "cold and frozen" items for last for obvious reasons. Less time out of the fridge makes the difference in whether you eat or drink your ice cream. Last, but certainly not least, give careful consideration to the time of day to prevent long delays on checkout lines. A swift departure is always an important part of a successful execution.

And of course let's not forget the creative shoppers—you know, the 50/12 club. Very often shoppers get pretty creative trying to rationalize how their 50 items really are only 12 items so they can get on the express lane. Once again, I'm sure you can relate to some or all of what I've described. Equally certain am I that there may have been several military operations that had less thought and preparation than these two previous examples. My goal here is to give you the right mind-set and break things down to their basic common denominator so you can feel as comfortable investing as you do shopping for your favorite item.

Now let's look at the "business professional"—you know, the very intense, critical thinkers. Well, as the old song line goes, "It ain't necessarily so." As long as they're in their everyday world, perhaps, "all systems are a go." However when it comes to investing, in most cases "Houston, we have a problem." They might as well be in a foreign country.

They also tend to be intimidated, or overwhelmed, and feel more comfortable handing off their money to someone else they hope is more qualified than they are to place those investment dollars successfully. They also feel if things go wrong, and they often do, they will have someone to blame. Unfortunately, in most cases investors don't even take the time to find an investment adviser who is well qualified to do the job. Therefore the only person they should be blaming is themselves. Here again, don't let those shopping skills go to waste.

Chapter 2

Don't Fall Victim to the "Sugar Rush"

"What is the sugar rush?" you ask! This brief true story about a friend of mine should illustrate my answer. Let's call him Mr. W. He's a successful restaurant owner who recently told me his tale of woe.

Mr. W was concerned about a recent stock market decline. His paper losses were mounting, the stock market scenario looked bleak, and his frustration and deep concern were apparent. He was coming to me for some hand-holding but more important for some real advice on a repair strategy. I first asked him how his restaurant business was doing. He told me business was great and that it was proceeding according to his plans. In fact, the first three years had been superb, with each year surpassing the previous one. Business had actually exceeded his greatest expectations.

Then I asked him to tell me what he did before he bought the restaurant and how he knew he should attempt to go forward. What insight did he have that told him this venture had the potential to be successful? He quickly replied that he first checked out the location, the potential competition, the initial cost and upkeep, and of course his potential for revenue to cover his expenses and provide a profit. O.K. That sounded pretty good, he apparently had done his homework.

He had a starting point; he then developed a blueprint, a design, and a sketch of how to reach the goal of having a successful, thriving restaurant. Then he executed his plan. Suffice it to say he made some good decisions or he wouldn't be where he is now. I then asked him to tell me what preparations he had carried out before he made his investments in the stock market.

His answers were not too startling. I had heard them many times before from others. He had selected a good stock that his wealthy boss owned, one his broker thought was going to triple, and one he had heard would be the next tech giant. In addition, the other stocks he purchased were also chosen based on suggestions from individuals with little or no knowledge of what the companies did or whether they were even profitable. Clearly, he hadn't done his homework. What happened to that element of critical thinking? The prudence, intellect, and perceptiveness he used to buy his restaurant were not utilized in his investing. It's not hard to see why one investment was successful and one failed miserably. He was a victim of the "sugar rush." This refers to the need for a quick start, or the sugar high you get when you want things to happen quickly. It is the need for fast results. But sugar highs come fast and leave fast, and invariably you are left with no nutritional value, or in this case no money. Acting on something without thinking it through is unwise. Put your brain in gear before you put your mouth in motion.

Unfortunately, Mr. W is not alone. Most investors jump into investing their hard-earned dollars or inheritance with a lottery mentality. Mr. W's situation is not an aberration. I know too many individuals who not only lost all of the gains they had accumulated in the "roaring 90s" tech rally but sadly much of their original principal, as well. Why? Simply stated, they did not have a game plan, and they wanted the quick fix. Another problem was that they didn't diversify. They most likely didn't know the best-kept secret I spoke of earlier, and quite frankly they were not really interested in even finding out about it.

Those investors jumped into the markets with the lottery mentality. Remember this, betting that markets will go up is *gambling,* not investing. Consider the following.

FOOD FOR THOUGHT

—If you "bet" on a horse at the track—we call it gambling.

—If you "bet" that you can pull a rabbit out of a hat—we call it entertainment.

—If you "bet" that a stock will go up—we call it investing.

DO YOU SEE A DIFFERENCE???—I HOPE SO!

The word "BET" is not a word that implies you are making a sound investment decision for you and your family. For instance do you invest money for your childs education or bet it? Do you invest money for your retirement or bet it? I think enough said, you get it by now.

Learn from Other People's Mistakes, It's a Lot Less Painful

When people are surveyed about investing, they invariably respond that they don't think they are capable of investing on their own or they don't have the time. They're capable; they're just not knowledgeable because nothing like this book has ever been written before. They think the professionals have all the answers and all the time to watch their investments. But most investment advisors have hundreds of accounts. How can they possibly devote enough time to all your personal needs? Don't underestimate yourself. Everyone has what it takes if they use the commonsense approach. Next to your house and your children's education, your investment dollars rank pretty high, I'm sure. Think about the time you will spend choosing the right house and/or college. Don't rush your investment dollars off too quickly. Give those dollars the right amount of time and thought.

Every profession has jokes and riddles written about it, and Wall Street is no exception. One such riddle is, Why did we create analysts? Answer: To make meteorologists look good. Another saying is that the same people who laugh at the thought of using fortune-tellers consistently listen to analysts.

And my personal favorite is that economists have predicted eight of the last four recessions.

Am I being too harsh? No, it comes with the territory. Let's just call them some interesting observations. In addition, there are a few more observations we should all make note of. First, no one has all the answers all the time. Second, we can agree that over time, markets will rise and fall as economic, political, and financial events interact. Therefore, we can surmise that if you agree on points one and two, no one could possibly predict when or how much the markets will move with any consistency because of all the variables. Why then should we put our trust and our money into someone's guess? Hence we must know how to prepare and plan not guess and bet.

Prepare, Don't Predict

Another point that everyone generally will agree on is that we all like to control as much of our own destiny as possible. If we agree on all those points, then let's prepare ourselves and take control of our own finances. Financial security provides a warm, cuddly feeling. I'm sure you don't want to hear from your advisor that she's right 90 percent of the time, and then find out you were in the other 10 percent.

When you are investing your hard-earned money—that which you finally get to keep after it's been taxed to death, that which you will be depending on for your retirement or that you will need for your child's college education—you had better be getting more for your money than a view of an investment counselor's plush office and a cup of coffee when you drop off your check.

My answer to those who say they don't have the time to do their own investing is *make* the time. Meet me halfway, and ask the right questions. Keep in mind that the answers come from the questions you ask, not from the so-called knowledge you think the other person has.

Take your time, don't rush into anything, and don't assume. Opinions are like noses. Everybody has one; some are good but many need work. When I'm planning for my children's education, I expect the money to be available in their freshman year, not when they're seniors. Prepare properly and you have less of a chance of needless surprises.

The seasons are a great example of why we should plan and prepare. Every year without fail, as summer draws to a close and fall approaches, squirrels begin gathering nuts. They are preparing themselves for winter. They know that it will be cold, but they don't know how cold. They know that snow will blanket the ground, but they don't know how much snow. They know storms will come, but they really don't know exactly when or how severe they will be. Nonetheless, they prepare for the worst. When you prepare for the worst, you minimize your possibilities for surprise. Squirrels instinctively know that many uncertainties exist, but if they prepare for a long, hard winter, they will minimize the possibility for surprise and hardship.

Winter has a certain time frame, so the squirrels will gather more than a sufficient supply of nuts to last through the winter months. Regardless of how severe or how mild the season ultimately is, they will have enough to survive. They prepare, they don't predict. We have to do the same. We have to invest based on appropriate planning to meet our goals and protect our investment over a long period of time.

In addition, we must have an exit strategy in case the tide turns unexpectedly. Finally, we must follow our plan so we have enough to outlast a financial storm and assure us that our nest egg will be there when we need it. We have to *prepare, not predict. Its never too early to start saving and no amount is too small to start with.*

Chapter 3

Get on the Bondwagon

I always start every conversation about investing by saying that *age equals percent of fixed income.* Most investors have little or no fixed income, let alone the proper amount. Hence, they're not diversified, or better stated they are severely underweighted in bonds. This is an accident waiting to happen. Bonds are the rudders of stability that keep your investments afloat.

Try sailing a boat without a rudder. Even if you don't sink, you'll float aimlessly. If you do reach your destination, it's purely by chance. Worse than that, you can't repeat the performance because you don't know how you got there in the first place. Oops, I just realized I said bonds. Well, I guess now you know my best kept secret—bonds. I will show you how you can easily incorporate them in your investment decisions.

Investors do poorly because they don't prepare. Instead, they try to predict, and they ignore the changes of the ever-evolving landscape. This book lists what I call the Ten Commitments to guide you and enable you to recognize when to leave the party, or stay longer.

If you're one of those investors that think it's too late to learn, start reading. It's never too late to learn what went wrong so you don't let it happen again. Keep in mind that unfortunately many individuals not only lost money in the 2008 disaster and the 1990s bubble but also are "repeat offenders" from the 1980s crash. They didn't research what went wrong the first time, and time faded their bad memories. By the time the 1990s rolled in, greed or the appearance of easy money took over. And when that happens, common sense gets pushed out. In 2008 there were similarities, another bubble. A different bubble perhaps, however all bubbles burst when they get too big. Do you know the definition of insanity? It's doing the same thing over and over again the same way each time and expecting different results. Something has to change.

You can begin your investment journey with three rules. Take the amount to be invested and proportion it this way.

CORNERSTONE RULES

1. AGE EQUALS PERCENT OF FIXED INCOME. INVEST REMAINDER IN STOCKS.

2. ALWAYS MAINTAIN THOSE PERCENTAGES AS TIME GOES ON.

3. NEVER FORGET RULES 1 AND 2.

These rules should be the cornerstones of your investment decisions. Be disciplined enough to carry them out and they will reward you handsomely.

Age equals percent of fixed income. Theoretically, let's say a 20-year-old has a greater life expectancy than someone who is 60. In addition, let's say that stocks are less predictable and therefore more volatile and consequently riskier than bonds. By using my formula, age equals percent of fixed income, we would recommend that a 20-year-old allocate 20 percent of his or her portfolio to bonds and the other 80 percent to stocks.

Conversely, a 60-year-old would begin with 40 percent allocated to stocks and 60 percent to bonds. This example alone illustrates how underweighted in fixed income most investors are.

Keep in mind when you are allocating percentages that a range is advisable, as shown in the following table. For instance, if someone is 22, we can use a range of 20 percent to 29 percent as the allotment for bonds, and an individual who is 63 could use a 60 to 69 percent allocation for bonds.

It's important to understand why we are using this method. The older you get, the closer you are to considering retirement with less time left to make up for bad markets and bad investments. The older you get, the more likely you are to want a secure nest egg. Therefore as you

Age Equals Percent of Fixed Income

Age	*Percentage of Fixed Income*
Under 20	10-20%
20-29	20-30%
30-39	30-40%
40-49	40-50%
50-59	50-60%
60-69	60-70%
70-79	70-80%
80-over	80-90%

get older, a higher percentage of your portfolio should be invested in a conservative tool that is more predictable and less volatile; hence, a larger portion should be allotted to fixed-income. Now that you know the right percentage, how do you figure out which bonds and stocks to buy?

Investing can be analogous to taking a car trip. Plan your journey properly, make sure you have the correct information, and allow yourself enough time to get there. Whether it's a vacation plan or a financial plan, the similarities are obvious. The operative word is *plan*. Before you embark on either kind of journey, ask yourself the following questions.

5 STEP PLAN FOR TRAVELING:

1. WHAT IS MY DESTINATION?
2. WHAT IS THE BEST WAY TO GET THERE?
3. WHAT IS AN ALTERNATE ROUTE IN CASE I ENCOUNTER SOMETHING UNEXPECTED?
4. HOW SHOULD I LAY OUT AND MAP MY PLAN OF ACTION, AND MONITOR MY PROGRESS?
5. WHAT IS MY TIME FRAME, AND WHAT ARE MY EXPECTATIONS?

Don't forget that investing takes time and thought. It's not a get-rich-quick scheme or a lottery. Every time you feel anxious or hurried, or each time you try to figure the best time to buy or sell, remember this phrase: Don't give me timing, give me time. You can't reach your destination any sooner by taking shortcuts or by playing the market. If you want to play something buy an instrument like a piano or a trumpet. I hear some people say they want to learn the tricks of the trade. My reply to them is that if they learn the trade, they won't need to look for any tricks.

Now, let's take the five steps for taking a trip that were mentioned earlier and apply them to our financial journey. Always keep in mind that investing is a journey in which direction is much more important than speed.

5 STEP PLAN FOR INVESTING:

1. What is your destination, or goal (e.g., a comfortable retirement, to provide a college education, income/wealth building)?
2. What vehicles should I use to reach my financial goals? (What percentage of stocks and bonds and what mix of maturity and rating should I seek for my bonds?)
3. Is there a way to change my course if an unexpected event occurs?
4. What amount should I invest initially and thereafter?
5. What is my risk tolerance? (Generally speaking, most investors are conservative, so risk should be minimized.)

If you keep your five steps as the background music and the following Ten Commitments as your road map, you will be headed in the right direction toward financial success.

The Ten Commitments

Next, as promised, I will outline the Ten Commitments. They will serve as your road map. You should refer to them regularly so you keep heading in the proper direction. All of them are explained in detail throughout the book.

    I.   Age equals the percentage of fixed income.
    II.   Prepare, don't predict.
    III.   Discipline yourself to invest. Don't speculate.
    IV.   Play sports or musical instruments, but don't play with the markets.
    V.   Spend more time watching your investments and less time watching T.V.
    V.   If a company is not making money, don't give them any of *your* money.
    VII.   When you buy bonds, invest in high-grade corporate bonds, municipal bonds, or U.S. Treasury issues.
    VIII.   If a company you are invested in starts to lose money, sell it.
    IX.   Don't buy high-yield bonds. High yield + High risk=Lost capital.
    X.   Reinvest dividends from stocks or interest from bonds into your stock allocation.

Review

1. Three cornerstone rules

2. Five step "plan of action"

3. The Ten Commitments road map

Earlier I mentioned 3 rules as the cornerstones of your investment decisions.

1. Age equals percent of fixed income (bonds) and invest the remaining percent in stocks (equities)

2. Always maintain those percentages

3. Never forget rule 1 and rule 2

What do I mean when I say those rules will be the cornerstones? Why are they so important? Taking the first step, age=% of fixed income easily sets the stage for all the rest of the steps you will take going forward. Its like marching. First step left next right and so on. Don't get out of step. When I say to maintain a balance between stocks and bonds, I don't necessarily mean equal amounts. I want you to buy an amount of the individual stocks or one of the three equity indexed trusts based on the age formula when you're allocating the equity portion of your portfolio. Too many investors reach for already packaged products like mutual funds and bond funds. Those funds usually have too many costs and charges that take away from your potential return.

It would be intellectually dishonest and totally inaccurate to use the argument that funds are professionally managed and therefore will outperform markets in good times and prevent losses during bad times. They generally go up and down just like the markets, so why pay all those charges? In addition, the high costs will take longer to absorb when stock prices rally (go up) and exacerbate your losses when prices decline.

To then suggest that it allows the investor to diversify is also overstated and exaggerated. You can diversify in other ways, which I will illustrate shortly, with significantly less cost. *Diversify* means "distribute carefully; balance in several ways." It doesn't mean buy everything you can get your hands on and pray.

I remember one man telling me that to him, global investing means you now get to lose your money internationally, not just domestically. With more than 10,000 funds, how are you going to figure out which one to buy? People invest for only a handful of reasons—income, retirement, and educational planning—so why then have 10,000 funds been created? In all fairness, I'm sure there are a handful that are well managed and have done well. But the complicated process of examining all the variations is exhausting for me. However that's your choice, or take mine, what I'm suggesting in this book.

If funds were the answer, why are so many combinations needed? Also in the vast majority of funds, the diversification being offered is really a multilayered collection of stocks in different sectors with no or little mention of bonds at all. A *balance of stocks and bonds that are based on your age* is the only way to go. That's why so many portfolios do poorly. They are too heavily weighted in stocks and severely underweighted in bonds. How can anyone claim to be diversified and completely exclude bonds from their portfolio? Bonds are necessary to balance the risk that stocks inherently have. Bonds have maturities which effectively take their market risk away, and you virtually take event risk out by adhering to a strict discipline of purchasing only high grade bonds or government issues.

Chapter 4

Choosing Stocks: As Easy as 1, 2, 3

Two Ways to Buy Equities

How do you select the right stocks? I have two answers for you. Either one works well.

Two methods can be used to acquire the equity portion of your portfolio. The first is the quick method, and the second is for the more cerebral individuals who prefer a little more hands on. If you want to know which one is better for you, ask yourself this question. When I buy an item that needs to be assembled, do I buy the item already assembled or do I take it home in the box and put together the product on my own?

The quick method takes less time; therefore, it can be more appealing to many who feel overcommitted with work, school, home, and children.

However, I must emphasize the importance of you choosing one or the other. Don't pass the decision off to someone else. The quick method is faster and gives you broader diversification right away. The long way focuses on the individual companies; therefore, it is slower, more time-consuming, and it offers less diversification initially. Either way, you will get the correct mix of stocks you need. More and more I find myself liking the quick method better. You might start with one method and do as others have done—combine a little of both. First buy one of the indexes and later on fill in with individual stocks. The quick method is an easier way to begin.

The quick method is a terrific way to enter the equity markets. You can participate in the three major stock market indexes, be diversified, and own only three securities. I'm referring to the DIAMONDS Trust, Series 1 (symbol DIA); the SPDR Trust, Series 1 (symbol SPY); and the Nasdaq-100 Trusts (symbol QQQ). All three are similar in structure and purpose. The Diamonds are an investment trust that holds a portfolio representing all 30 stocks in the Dow Jones Industrial Average (DJIA). Diamonds shares are priced and traded throughout the day, similar to common stocks.

Your ownership in Diamonds shares will move up and down proportionately with the DJIA. Similarly, the SPDR Trust, also referred to as spiders, is a trust that holds all of the common stocks of the S&P 500 Composite Stock Price Index. The SPDR price also will generally correspond to the price performance of the S&P 500 Index.

Lastly, the Nasdaq-100 trust represents ownership interest in the Nasdaq-100. Once again, investment results will generally correspond to the price performance of the component securities of the Nasdaq-100 indexes. All three are easy to trade, easy to follow, and an effective way to diversify.

Before investing, take a look at a list of the companies that make up each index. You may choose to buy one, two or all three. In the back of this book are listed all the stocks that make up all 3 indexes.

My preference is to always start by owning representation in the DJIA, so I would first put 50 percent of my equity investment in the Diamonds shares. (The DJIA is often referred to as the old economy stocks.) Although changes occur periodically, I am including a complete list of all the stocks in each one of the three indexes so you can get an idea of the diversity you will have. I would invest the other 50 percent of my equity money in each of the remaining two.

So, using this example, if the initial equity portion of your investment were $1,000, you would invest $500 in the Diamonds index trust, and the other $500 would be divided between the Nasdaq-100 and the SPDR.

When choosing individual stocks of companies, you begin with the same decision you face when buying any other item: You decide whether or not you like it. I don't like to choose stocks based on ratios or analysts' predictions of earnings or future sales. Generally speaking, I believe their opinions are far too optimistic, and their opinions vary dramatically based on the periods of time they use. Also keep in mind most predictions are based on assumptions. We all know what assumptions do!

I prefer to look at a company's bottom line. What is the company's net income? Are they making money or not? If they are making money, then we go to step two; if not, we look for another company.

You first select them based on your observations and experiences. What kind of car do you drive? What type of computer do you have? Who manufactures your clothing and jewelry, and which stores sell those products? Next, look around. You don't live on an oasis. Do many other people share your taste in cars, household items, clothing, food, computers, and so on?

Take a few names from the list and research whether these companies are actually making money. It is also important that these companies have been making money for at least two years. Does that sound like absurdly obvious advice? I can't begin to tell you how many people invest in companies that they have never heard of. In addition, they don't know where the companies are located or what they do, and they don't have a clue whether they currently make a profit, let alone what the company's future prospects are. Once you have a few names you can begin your stock purchases with the proper allocation mentioned earlier (age equals percent of fixed income, the remainder in stocks).

We want to purchase stocks of companies worthy of your investment dollars. If the company doesn't have a track record of making money, why would you want to give them yours?

After you have researched the company and find the one you like, you must monitor the financials regularly. Compare it to buying a car. You choose what you like based on shopping around. After buying it, you periodically check the oil, get gas, and bring it in for service. It's the same for stocks. Stocks require upkeep, monitor the company periodically, when and if things change, evaluate whether to keep it or move on to something else. Again, if a company isn't making money, don't give them yours.

This is why many individuals get into trouble. They buy into start-up companies that have a lot of promises and good intentions. All too often though, these companies run into unforeseen snags and can't meet their expectations. They're forced to reevaluate, and many never make it. Let them work out the kinks on their money, not yours. Then you can take a look. It's like a new model car. Never buy it the first year. Let others test-drive it and get those kinks out before you make a purchase.

Next we want to determine how much money to start with. It does not take a lot of money to start. Many companies are in the $20 to $75 a share range, so you can buy small amounts. If you add to those purchases on subsequent special days, over time you will buy yourself and/or your children a fine nest egg. You can enter the market with a lump sum or with incremental amounts periodically.

For instance, an excellent way to start investing in individual stocks is to use the monthly investment method. The monthly investment method works like this. Instead of buying the stock of each company you choose all at once, you buy it over time. You do this by taking an equal amount of the money you will be investing and purchase the same dollar amount of the stock on the same day each month for six months.

Let's say you choose a $50 stock and you have $1,000 to invest. If you buy it all at once, you will buy 20 shares of stock. If you use the monthly investment method, you will invest approximately $167 per month for six months for a total amount of $1,000.

When the stock is selling at $50, you will buy approximately three shares each month. If the stock falls to $40, you will buy four shares. If, on the other hand, the stock goes to $70, you will buy only two shares.

The purpose of the monthly investment method is to get an average price over a six-month period by buying fewer shares when the stock is higher in price and more shares when the stock is lower in price. Some monthly investments are made over a twelve-month period. Both work the same way. Pick a day of the month that's easy to remember and try to buy the stock at around the same time of the day you have chosen.

There are three easy steps to follow for each stock you buy.

1. Before you buy a stock, research whether the company has made money for at least two consecutive years.

2. After you own a stock, check to see that each quarter's earnings are equal to or higher than the previous one.

3. If earnings drop for two consecutive quarters, sell and look for something else.

Do not start thinking that this will take too much time. Your money is at stake. It takes discipline to invest wisely. It takes common sense to figure out your money is more important to you than it is to anyone else.

At times, you might have to leave the party early due to unforeseen events. That's a problem that most investors have. They know how to buy, but they don't know when to sell. All too often, individuals as well as professionals look at extensive formulas and ratios to prove different theories. Others look at increased sales as an indicator of good things to come. However, if a company increases its sales without reducing the costs of production, it will lose even more money.

When the price of a stock is falling or the stock is selling off, there's a reason. Sometimes it can be attributed to a minor correction in the marketplace, but sometimes it's the start of a sustained drop. Sustained drops often have several small, periodic upticks along the way. I call them head fakes.

That's why the rule about two consecutive quarters of negative earnings is a red flag and a warning that the price of the stock has been running faster than the earnings. That's why I think it's a sell sign. The price of the stock must justify the earnings. If the price runs up too fast and earnings don't move higher, a price retreat must take place to get them back in line. If the earnings don't hold their levels, the stock price will fall again and so on until a balance is met.

If earnings start to move up, that will also have a stabilizing effect on the stock, and once again a balance will be achieved. Although this is not an exact science, the ratios that everyone else is showing you aren't either. The difference is that these are real-time numbers, not future sales, earnings, or other numbers based on expectations that are virtually never predicted correctly and often adjusted. When things change, there is a reason. You must recognize it, adapt, and overcome. Remember the comparison of taking a trip I gave you earlier? I said have an alternative plan in case you need to take a detour. The point is simply this: If a company doesn't make money, it eventually will fail.

End of story!

The phrase, I'm losing money but I'm making it up in volume, is a sarcastic remark not an investment strategy. To buy such a company's stock is probably not sound investment advice. Buying a stock because it dropped significantly is also not a sound reason for you to run out and buy it. I hear that comment very often, after a stock's price falls. It must be a buy. Why? How do you know it won't go lower? Again, a classic case of betting and calling it investing.

First, find out why it dropped so much. Typically, there's a good reason: poor sales, management problems, or little or no profit margin. These types of problems are not fixed quickly, so get out before the problems worsen.

Since these types of headaches don't go away quickly, it's as the saying goes—time to leave the party early before things get out of hand.

It would be wiser to wait until the company shows signs of turning around and making money again before you leap in. No one knows what the very bottom is until you hit it, so why have your money tied up for an indefinite period of time waiting? I can guarantee you this. If you don't take my advice and do the research beforehand, you will get stuck with a bad position in a failing company. By then it's too late.

Chapter 5

Balance Risk

Let's consider the bond side. Corporate bonds are simply long-term IOUs issued by major corporations. Maturities range from 1 year to as long as 100 years.

Generally speaking, corporate bonds pay a fixed rate of return until maturity, then at maturity the issuer repays the bond's principal. Bonds have three major components—rating, coupon, and maturity—that enable you to pick the right bond for each objective. The rating of a bond will set the tone and gauge its quality.

Triple A (or AAA) is the highest of the investment grades and triple B (or BBB) is the lowest of the investment-grade bonds. Everything below BBB is referred to as high yield, or more commonly just called junk. The accompanying table lists how the two major rating services display risk/quality.

Credit Ratings

Credit Risk	Moody's	Standard & Poors
Investment Grade		
Highest quality	Aaa	AAA
High quality (very strong)	Aa	AA
Upper medium grade (strong)	A	A
Medium grade	Baa	BBB
Not Investment Grade		
Lower medium grade (Somewhat speculative)	Ba	BB
Low grade (speculative)	B	B
Poor quality (may default)	Caa	CCC
Most speculative	Ca	CC
No interest being paid or	Could	C bankruptcy petition filed
In default	D	D

This chart is just a guide so you can see the wide variety of ratings there are. My suggestion is only stay with the stronger ratings. The reasoning for that is simple—Bonds are meant to balance risk in your portfolio, not add to it. The rating you choose depends on your risk tolerance; again, a bond is supposed to be used to balance risk, not add more. Therefore I would suggest that you use U.S. Treasury notes and bonds or AAA, AA, or high-quality, A-rated corporate bonds.

Next, bonds have different coupons, or interest payments, that indicate the cash flow that the investor will be receiving periodically over the life of the bond, usually semiannually or monthly. The coupon is a result of where interest rates are at the time of issuance. Let's suppose interest rates are currently at 5 percent for bonds rated AAA. That means that for every $1,000 bond you buy, you will receive 5 percent per year, or $50 of interest income per year, usually paid semiannually. In this example, you would get $25 per bond every six months on the specific interest payment date. If you purchased five bonds (also written 5m) you would receive $50 per bond in interest, multiplied by five bonds, for a total of $250 of income annually.

If the bonds had a five-year maturity, you would receive a total of $1,250 in income over the five years. At the specific maturity date, you also would get your original $5,000 principal returned.

It's important to note that as long as you hold the bond until maturity, you will eliminate any market risk. All too often, investors think that if they buy a bond and interest rates go up, the bonds will go down in price. Certainly on paper that is so; however, regardless of where interest rates are when your bonds mature, you will get all of your principal back.

Zero coupon bonds have all of the other features of their fixed-coupon cousins except that they pay no periodic interest. Hence, they are called zero (0) coupon bonds. Instead, they are issued at a deep discount and at mature you receive $1,000, the same way coupon bonds do. Your return is based on the difference between the deep discount and par ($1,000).

As mentioned earlier, bonds have a maturity, a date in the future when you get your principal back, which is your initial investment, usually $1,000 face per bond. The fact that a bond matures is important because it takes out the market volatility risk inherent in most other investments. Maturities can range from 1 year to 100 years. This wide range makes bonds an excellent planning vehicle.

The issuer will pay back your principal regardless of where interest rates are at the time your bond matures. You can virtually take out the event risk (credit risk, rating changes) by buying only the highest ratings, or U.S. Treasury notes or bonds.

What maturity do you get, and how many bonds should you purchase? That depends on the investment objective *de jour*.

Finally, don't buy high-yield bonds!

High-yield bonds are commonly called junk bonds. Now I ask you do you want to put your hard-earned money into something called *junk?* Think of all the things you refer to as junk and consider whether anything worthwhile comes to mind. Doctors don't tell you to eat junk food, and you don't furnish your house at the junkyard. You don't want to add any unnecessary risk to your portfolio, so keep the junk out of it, too. Always remember that you are buying stocks for growth and bonds for income and stability.

A junk bond is basically a stock on steroids. It looks like a bond because it has a coupon and a maturity date. However, the rating is clearly below the investment-grade level. Even the way a junk bond trades will signal that it's different. Virtually all high-grade, quality corporate bonds trade on a yield spread over Treasury bonds. That's the way the bond's value is determined. A junk bond typically trades on a dollar price basis, just like a stock. Stay away, wrong way, go back, STOP! Only high-grade bonds allowed.

The rating of a junk bond gives it away. Junk bonds have a below-investment-grade rating which means the likelihood of receiving your coupon payment is questionable. Without a coupon, there can be no yield. That's why they are referred to as junk. If the rating is still investment grade and the yield is much higher than similarly rated bonds, it raises another flag. If a typical baa/bbb-rated bond is, for example, 200 basis points or 2 percent higher than Treasury bonds and you see a comparable issue plus 300 basis points or more, there's a reason. You'll no doubt get someone to tell you how much yield you *could* or *would* get if the coupon gets paid. The problem is that it might not pay at all. In addition, if they're not paying the coupon, the price of your bond will probably drop 50 percent to 75 percent, which means there's a good chance that in addition to not getting your interest payment, you will not be getting most or all of your principal back anytime soon or at maturity. Don't take short cuts, or your investment could be cut short.

There's an expression that comes to mind as very appropriate at this time. "THERE ARE NO FREE LUNCHES." If you think something looks too good to be true, it probably isn't what you think. Take a second look and ask plenty of questions. The marketplace, especially the bond market, is very efficient. With that in mind, if a yield looks too good or too high for the rating, there's a reason and it's usually not a good one. Junk bonds often appeal to investors who are not doing well in the stock market, so they look to the bond market as an alternative. You don't want to replace one bad bet with another.

Investors should be looking to create a balance, not create an alternative. Remember age equals percent of fixed income, or bonds. Sometimes investors who haven't done well are looking to make up a loss in a hurry and see the junk bond market as a way to do that. Initially, they take the conventional look and interpret high-grade yields as too low for them. They need more yield and more excitement, and look out, here comes the sugar rush.

This is how such investors think they will make up for lost time and lost money—fast. They see the high-yield market and decide to give it a try. Unfortunately, they don't see risk and don't want to see risk. In most cases, you can't talk them out of their decision to go ahead, even when you explain the pitfalls. Unfortunately, like the moth drawn to the flame, their investments go up in a ball of smoke . . . Don't be in denial . . . Remember D-NILE is a river in Egypt.

Chapter 6

Certificates of Deposit a.k.a CDs

The bank CERTIFICATE OF DEPOSIT or CD for short is a basic staple of products that are offered by banks to their depositors. Most people I think are pretty familiar with the usual characteristics and structure of CDs that banks usually have posted on wall posters, free standing signs or brochures on the various counters scattered all around the bank. The basic structure of CDs are:

1 - A defined period of time or duration that you must hold it. [a maturity date] Usually a few months to a few years.

2 - A penalty for withdrawal prior to the maturity date.

3 - Some CDs allow pre-mature withdrawal without penalty, however they will typically offer you a lower rate of interest for that option.

4 - A fixed rate that is typically higher than a usual bank deposit rates.

5 - A specific dollar amount per CD purchased.

6 - The amount of your deposit is FDIC insured up to the amount the law allows. Currently, it is $250,000 per depositor. FDIC [Federal Deposit Insurance Corporation]. Keep in mind that the FDIC insurance insures up to $250,000 including interest earned. So, take that into account when purchasing CDs. Purchase less that the $250,000 to accommodate the amount of interest you will be earning.

All of these facts should always be checked and confirmed with the bank you are dealing with before you purchase a CD. You should also check various banks since interest rates can vary dramatically from bank to bank. Also, ask and be clear that what is being offered is what you are getting. Sometimes a teaser rate is only good for a short time and then a lesser rate kicks in for the remainder of the time left. Ask about hidden fees if any. Lastly, be clear that RENEWALS are OPTIONAL and that NO AUTOMATIC renewals can be done. You should only accept a renewal after you have been properly NOTIFIED in enough time before the maturity date so you can APPROVE the new duration and new interest rate being offered. If you do not like the new terms you can withdraw the proceeds without any fees or penalties.

ONE TIP ON PURCHASING CDs—Ladder your maturities. Instead of taking $250,000 and buying one CD, with a single maturity buy 5 different CDs with 5 different maturities. For instance lets say I have $250,000 and want to buy a CD. I am not sure what maturity to buy, I am not sure if I will need some of the money within the next few years. So, I can divide the $250,000 into 5 different maturities of $50,000 each. I then can scale or ladder the maturities equally from 1 year out to 5 years. Now I have $50,000 maturing every year for the next 5 years. I am receiving a different rate of interest for each year and typically the longer I go out in maturity the higher the rate. Every time one matures, I can either use it for expenses, recreation, buy real estate or just reinvest it in a new CD or another investment opportunity. If I chose to buy another CD, I can continue the ladder by purchasing a 5 year maturity hence my 1,2,3,4,5 ladder stays intact.

Up until now I have only been discussing Bank CDs. Brokerage firms also offer CDs. All of the questions you should ask a bank representative that I mentioned earlier should be applied here as well. Brokerage firm CDs in many ways are similar to bank CDs. They have stated durations, fixed rates of interest for the period of time you want and usually are FDIC insurance.

The major difference is in a brokerage firm you will get more choices. They will have many more issuers to chose from. If you have larger sums to invest, that $250,000 limit can be handled more efficiently in one place with many choices rather than going from bank to bank.

MONEY
SECURITIES
CREDIT
FORECLOSURE
MORAL HAZZARD
GLOBAL
INVESTMENT
FINANCIAL
CRISIS
LIABILITY
BANKRUPTCY
BANKING
DEBT
STOCK
BONDS
CASH
BANK RUN
CURRENCY
REAL ESTATE
LIQUIDITY
SUB-PRIME
LOSS
RISK
BUBBLE
STAGFLATION
INTEREST RATES
DEVALUE
LEVERAGE
DEFAULT LOANS
INSOLVENCY
ECONOMY
DERIVATIVES
ASSET
MARKET CRASH
RECESSION
COLLATERAL
MORTGAGES
CAPITAL
PROPERTY
COLLAPSE
INFLATION

Chapter 7

How Much Should My Initial Investment Be?

It's Not About Stocks "OR" Bonds
It's About Stocks "AND" Bonds

We talked earlier about the right balance of stocks and bonds (age equals percent of fixed income or bonds). The first step to investing is to open an account with a reputable brokerage firm by depositing your initial amount in their money market fund.

Usually amounts of $500 to $1,000 are the minimum requirements, although smaller amounts can often be accommodated.

The best way to add to this initial amount is to make additional deposits monthly. The important thing is to be disciplined and do it on a certain day each month. Remember the saying: Pay yourself first.

The proceeds that you deposit in this account will ultimately be used to purchase your stocks and bonds. Now you're ready to start. If you choose the quick method (buying the index versus individual stocks), ask your broker for the current price of the DIA, QQQ, or the SPY and use the percentage of your proceeds allotted for stocks to purchase shares of one or all of the indexes.

Then, based on the type of bonds you decided to buy (U.S. Treasury, corporate, or municipal), use your bond allocation to start building your laddered bond portfolio of one-to five-year maturities. Again, if you don't have enough to do this all at once, it's okay to start building gradually.

Let me give you an example of how one couple started and continued to build an excellent portfolio.

Mr. and Mrs. Z had $6,000 to invest. They were in their mid 40s and had no previous experience investing in the markets.

They started by building a laddered bond portfolio of one-to five-year maturities in U.S. Treasury notes. (See charts on following page for illustration.)

They bought bonds with maturities of one year, two years, three years, four years, and five years. Each bond cost approximately $1,000. With the remaining $1,000, they chose to buy shares of the DIAMONDS Trust, Series 1 (DJIA), which, as mentioned earlier, is based on an investment trust that holds a portfolio representing all 30 DJIA stocks.

The amount of shares purchased will vary depending on the price per share at the time of purchase. The bonds they purchased had coupons that paid interest directly to the brokerage account periodically. When the interest payments were credited, they used the proceeds to purchase additional shares of DIA. This is a conservative portfolio and fulfills their needs and probably the needs of many others as well, simply because it accomplishes what most investors want—*preservation of principal and a good rate of return.* As they grow older they will of course have to increase their percentage of fixed income investments.

Another option is to invest the coupon from the bond to buy stocks if you prefer purchasing individual stocks instead of an index. I've seen investors do what I call "I like the stock, I like the bond." Some investors who particularly like a company will buy a high-grade corporate bond for their bond allocation and use the coupon interest from that bond to purchase stock of the same company. This way, the bond is providing the steady flow of income, and the stock is providing an opportunity for growth.

Another example of how to incorporate bonds in your investments is college planning. If you are saving to pay for a child's college education, you will need a designated amount at the beginning of each year for at least four years (freshman, sophomore, junior, and senior years).

Let's say your child is presently 5 years old. The freshman year of college usually begins at 18 years of age; hence, we can start building a sequential maturity or ladder of bond maturities beginning with a 13-year maturity first, a 14-year maturity next, then a 15-year, and a 16-year maturity to finish up, as shown in the following figure.

Basic Ladder Structure*

4 senior	2030 maturity	THE
3 junior	2029 maturity	BASIC
2 sophomore	2028 maturity	LADDER
1 freshman	2027 maturity	STRUCTURE

*The basic ladder refers to any group of sequential maturities.

U.S. Treasury zero coupon bonds are generally your best bet for this type of investment. You can start by purchasing small amounts because zeros trade at deep discount prices. In addition, the easily accessible Treasury marketplace makes multiple small purchases easy.

This type of structure can be used in many ways, and the possible combinations of maturities and amounts are endless. The other form of ladder is called the rollover, as shown in the following figure.

The Rollover*	
5-year maturity	4-year maturity
4-year maturity	3-year maturity
3-year maturity	2-year maturity
2-year maturity	1-year maturity
1-year maturity	This bond matures

*Rollover refers to continuously reinvesting maturing bonds to maintain the five-year structure.

The rollover structure is similar to the straight ladder, but it generally is used as a basic fixed-income tool to balance stock portfolios. Regular interest-bearing bonds (bonds with a coupon) or zero coupons can be used in a rollover. We start the ladder going out one year and then add a second, third, fourth, and fifth year in sequential order. At the end of the first year, the first issue will mature, the second bond will become first, the third maturity date will be second, and so on.

When the first bond matures, those proceeds can be used to buy a new bond with a five-year maturity to keep the five-year sequence going.

When the second bond matures the following year, you use those proceeds to buy another five-year maturity bond, and so on and so on, keeping at all times the five-year integrity. The rollover is an excellent way to invest in the bond market. It allows the investor to avoid market fluctuations due to interest rate changes that cause bonds to move in wide ranges.

Bonds mature regardless of where interest rates are. In the aforementioned scenario, if interest rates are higher, you can take the proceeds from the maturing bond and buy the five-year maturity with a higher yield than the one that matured. If interest rates are lower, only 20 percent of your portfolio is being invested at the lower rate. In both cases, your bond matures and no loss is incurred. That is just one of the valuable qualities of a bond—it matures.

That quality alone is why bonds are an invaluable planning vehicle and a must for all portfolios.

Planning for a child's education properly now is like watching your diet and nutritional intake. The benefits derived from such actions today are modest compared to the priceless return you will receive in the future. Financial health and personal well-being go hand in hand. It is easy to draw a parallel between the two. Just observe how people now more than in previous generations embrace the concept of a better lifestyle.

People today pay attention to calories, cholesterol, weight, type of food they eat, and water intake. It seems like no one can make a move these days without a bottle of water. Many also have a physical fitness regimen, and others at least attempt to stay active. This coupled with advances in medicine has resulted in an increase in our life expectancy rates. Therefore, financial well-being is even more essential and will be even more important so that we can fund our extended longevity.

Remember what I said about your child's education. Unlike previous generations, most of our children will go to college. After the cost of your home, a college education probably will be your biggest expense. Hence, long-term savings and planning are absolutely necessary.

So don't put things off, and don't speculate or gamble with your family's future.

In every exercise or diet regimen, *you* must participate; no one else can do it for you. The same is true when you invest. You have to get involved and only employ some help to *assist* you. Don't leave it all to someone else.

Don't think that only someone in the financial services business can build a successful portfolio. You are capable. I believe that most advisers are trying to get you good results; however, in many cases they use packaged products too quickly. I think most advisers are generalists, not specialists, and packaged products are their answer. In addition, advisers have many clients. How are they going to keep track of hundreds of clients who have situations that are changing periodically in a moving marketplace? They can't. You're the only one who can move quickly in your ever-changing world. Therefore, if you learn how to use the tools of the trade, you can build a stronger financial future for yourself and your family.

You can use advisers for the purchase and sale of your securities or for the use of research data. But *you* should choose what to buy and sell.

Many advisers, consultants, and salespersons are also unsure of their choices, and in many cases they are not as knowledgeable as they would like to be in all the products their firm has to offer.

Therefore, they take the easy way out and default to packaged products. You should be looking for advice, direction, and experience—not excuses. Putting together individual stocks and bond portfolios like I am suggesting takes a little more time. But what's the hurry? That's what advisers get paid for. Preparing a gourmet meal takes time too, and I think my money should be treated like a gourmet meal, not fast food. Don't you?

I want good food, not fast food, and so do you; we both know it's healthier. Prepackaged products have too much built-in cost, charges, fees, or whatever the professionals want to call it. You can be sure their services are not totally free.

Nothing is wrong with paying a reasonable commission. Just make sure you get what you pay for—advice and time. I'm not suggesting that individual purchases are commission free, but they generally are more reasonable.

An adviser should, as the word suggests, be advising you. If they call themselves brokers—well you know what word is in the word broker. All kidding aside, assistance is what you need as long as *you* lead the way. To help avoid seeing only packaged products, ask your adviser for individual stock and bond suggestions in the proportions mentioned earlier based on your age.

Perhaps you are thinking that you still don't know how to choose your own stocks and bonds. If you have ever bought a car, a house, or a suit of clothes, then you can do this, too. Did you have to know how to build or make each product you have purchased? When you eat good food, do you have to know how to grow it or even cook it? Investing is the same. When building a portfolio, learn what the building blocks are—the right balance and the correct proportions. And remember, investing is not a spectator sport. You can do it. Just try.

Chapter 8

Kids Can Have Fun Investing, Too

**Teach Them to Save. Trust Me,
Spending They Will Learn on Their Own**

A great way to approach kids about investing is the same way you approach adults—you find out their likes and dislikes. After all, adults are just kids who got older. I ask kids what they like to eat; what soft drinks they prefer; and what candy, cake, or ice cream they love. The answers will no doubt flow quickly. Based on those questions, kids will invariably mention at least a dozen companies that issue stock that they can purchase. I then ask them if they would like to know how they could own a portion of those companies.

When you buy a stock, you are purchasing shares that represent ownership in a company. Children always respond in awe and surprise at the notion that they, in fact, can own a part of such companies. This is the start of a future of saving money, and at the same time it means investing in companies and contributing to the welfare of our financial marketplace.

Think back to when you were a kid. If you had used this approach, what stocks would you now own, how many shares might you have, and what would they be worth? If you play this type of game and make it fun, it's educational and informative, and it shows kids how to save money. They can also make it part of a gift list for a sibling, and you can make it part of a gift for your kids and the children of friends and relatives.

How many times have you said or heard people say that they don't know what to buy for so and so? How many times have you defaulted to the old standby, the savings bond? Savings bonds are better than not investing at all. However, now I think you have much more to go with, more to have fun with, more to choose from, more to teach with, and a better chance to remember where it all is. Those savings bonds always seem to wind up in the oddest places. Kidding aside, buying stocks for kids and getting them involved is invaluable. It's ongoing because it grows with them. You can buy shares on their birthday and add to the amount each subsequent year. You can buy two shares, then three, and so on. You can add to the same company or diversify, as they get older. The ways to invest in stocks are endless, and the results are awesome.

In addition to an introduction to saving and investing, this could also spark a flame for a future interest in a possible occupation. Many good things can come from simply asking that first question: What are your favorite foods, soft drinks, and sweets?

Joseph A. Castelluccio, Jr.

Investing Is a Journey, Not a Destination

Here's a fable that illustrates the mystery of finding the elusive answer to the age-old question of the financial markets. There once was an old man who lived in California. He took strolls along the beach each day. One day on his walk, he came across a shiny object that had been left in the wake of a huge wave. When he picked it up, he was amazed to find that it was a bottle with what appeared to be a small person inside. He popped open the cork and was shocked to see that the small person in the bottle was in fact a life-sized genie who immediately appeared before him.

Most grateful to the old man for releasing him, the genie granted the old man a wish for anything he wanted. The old man thought for a while and said, "Well, I don't like to fly in planes and I always wanted to go to Hawaii. Could you build me a bridge that would connect California and Hawaii so I could drive there?"

The genie pondered the request and responded, "That's a real tough request—practically impossible. The span for that distance has never been done. Even if I did manage to get a bridge up. I'm not sure it would stay up. Isn't there possibly something else you would want that I could more easily do?"

The old man though again and said, "Oh yes. I know what you can do for me. I've always wanted to know more about stocks. You know, how to figure out the stock market fluctuation so I know when the best time to buy and sell is."

The genie looked at the old man and seriously pondered his second request. Then, without further hesitation, he confidently replied, "Let's go back to the bridge. Do you want two lanes or four?"

Chapter 9

The Generic Person

A Walk-Through of an Investor's Lifetime

"Generic Person" is a representation of an investor's life. The steps and stages are ones that can be generally expected. This chapter will present the time line of investing for Generic Person. Our lives are like a book, they have a beginning, a story, and an end. There are various chapters that separate the different segments of our lives. The many pages give the details that tie it all together, so the story has meaning. The generic person will walk us through the different chapters of a person's investment life, show you the stops along the way, and emphasize the shifts in balance that you should make.

When it comes to peoples' likes and dislikes, we may be different in many ways, but when it comes to our investment life, the process of investing is quite similar. We parallel each other in every walk of life.

Although we follow different career paths, our lives all have the same linear path. Regardless of who you are, no matter how rich or poor, you're born, get educated, work, and retire, getting older along the way. Many of us fill in the gaps with a family and a few job changes, but that aside, we are all on the same biological clock. The book of life goes on for approximately 30,000 days. The average novel is only about 250 pages. So, as you can see, you need to plot your course, be patient, and make adjustments so that financial security will not only be there in the later chapters but on every page along the way.

Generic Person is born, and for the first 10 years, he or she has birthday parties and receives holiday gifts and presents for special occasions. Many of these gifts are in the form of cash. This is the beginning of the accumulation process. In the pioneer days, we were all hunters and gatherers; during this particular time, we gather. The cash we gather is deposited into bank accounts and money market accounts, always hunting for the best rate of return among the banks and brokerage accounts. Stock purchases or investments in the stock index funds mentioned earlier (DIA, SPY, or the QQQ) could be made as cash accumulates. Again, it is a personal choice whether to go with individual stocks or the indexes. At this point, your concentration is focused mainly on the equity markets, since risk is less of a concern at early ages. Between the ages of 10 and 20, Generic Person is growing physically, mentally, and financially.

Those special occasions keep coming; the financial growth, which looked small and insignificant at the start, is showing some promise, and the stock purchases are building nicely. At this point, we begin to make our bond purchases. Remember, *age equals the percent of fixed income,* which refers to bonds. For this reason, as more cash is accumulated, we begin to make bond purchases to get a balance of approximately 10 percent to 20 percent of our total investment in bonds and the remainder in stocks or stock indexes. Suppose we had

$10,000 invested in stocks; we would put the next $2,000 into bonds. Between the ages of 20 and 30, we continue to make stock and bond purchases; however, by this time, Generic Person could have as much as 30 percent of the total investments in bonds.

This is a critical point because most individuals are severely underweighted in bonds. That is why most investors get into trouble—they rarely have bonds, and if they do, it's not the right amount or percentage of the total investment.

If Generic Person stays single or gets married and doesn't have children, the process continues and the bond percentages continue to increase periodically. However, if Generic Person does have children, a minor detour occurs. One must begin the aforementioned process for Generic Baby and at the same time maintain the balances for Generic Person's investments as time moves on.

It's important to start early because the clock starts ticking the day a baby is born. Starting early also will instill good savings habits for your children. Believe me when I say that they learn at a young age how to spend money on their own. You have to teach and they have to learn how to save money.

When it comes time to send them off to college, you'll be glad you started saving early. College costs rise constantly. Time moves faster than you think—one minute they're calling you Mommy and Daddy and the next minute they're calling you collect. I'm sure you can chew gum and walk at the same time, so I'm sure you'll be able to handle both investment portfolios simultaneously.

There is a pattern to the investing-accumulate funds, buy equities, add bonds based on age to balance your portfolio, and as interest income from your bonds grows, purchase additional equities.

For each child, begin the process the same way. If you have no children, concentrate solely on your own investments. Eventually, you reach the golden years when your portfolio should be around 70 percent to 80 percent in bonds with the balance in stocks. Those of you that have children will now be in a position to hopefully start funding—you guessed it—Generic Grandchild. But by now you're a pro at it. You'll be quite satisfied to find that at this time, instead of worrying about the stock market gyrations, you'll be collecting coupons (an expression for interest income from bonds in the days when you clipped the coupons and brought them to a bank for redemption) from your substantial bond portfolio. Now of course you are either mailed a check or your account is credited. Many investors at this point may even opt for 100 percent bonds, because it is just one less thing to worry about. With many chapters left in your book of life, you might as well spend the time enjoying it.

Chapter 10

How To Get Out Of Debt

The best way to get out of debt is of course to never get into debt in the first place. That said, the reality is that many people start out with good intentions and unfortunately get caught up in the "want it now", instant gratification mode and wind up way in over their heads. It often begins many times with what appears to be an innocent offer by a credit card company sending you a credit card that you didn't ask for. They offer you a zero interest rate for a period of time and a modest credit limit you can spend up to. You try it out, get the statement and pay the low minimum payment required. That's it, you're hooked. That goes on awhile and they say, something like "because you are such a valued customer we're upping your limits. Part flattered, part pleased with yourself, you gladly accept. Of course you are still sending the minimum payment thinking you are doing everything right and not noticing at the same time the grace period for zero interest rate on the balance has run out. Now the fun starts because you are using the higher credit limits they gave you and your balances are much higher. In addition you are now getting charged some ridiculous interest rates certainly over zero, often 20%+ on the new higher balance. In most cases the payments you are making don't even cover or barely cover the interest charge, hence if you continue to send the minimum payment you will virtually never be able to pay it off. In fact the balance you owe will go even higher even if you don't buy another thing. This is the beginning of the end because by this time too many people have several credit cards and this process is occurring on all of them, eventually putting you into a serious state of affairs that will jeopardize your financial health and your physical well being also. This happens to people of every age, gender and race. Understand, credit card companies give as many people as possible the equal opportunity to pay outrageous rates. In the words of Mark Twain, "a banker is a fellow who lends you his umbrella when the sun is shining, but wants it back the minute it begins raining".

So, what is one to do? What can be done when you receive these cards? First and foremost credit cards used properly are a necessary evil to establish a credit rating via a credit report. When you want to buy a house a good credit report with a good credit score will be extremely beneficial in obtaining a favorable interest rate on the amount you are borrowing. Hence, a better interest rate on your mortgage will save you thousands of dollars over the life of the mortgage therefore enhancing your monthly cash flow. So, lets get back to the original question, "What can be done when someone receives these credit cards with enticing terms"? The answer is different for everyone. The following question has to be answered. Do you have any credit cards before this one came? If the answer is "yes", I have 1 or more credit cards than don't accept it. If the answer is "no" then you should consider it. We all need at least one card, because we're not always walking around with cash and a

The Investor's Survival Guide

credit card is handy to have in that case. However, only use that card for the dollar amount of purchases that you will be able to pay back in its ENTIRETY when your statement comes in the mail. Don't get duped into thinking you can afford more than you need because the card is easier to use than actually counting dollar bills. Even if you have to take a moment and envision yourself actually counting cash, do it to slow the process. You need to discipline yourself before you enter the store that the credit card you will using will be limited to a certain amount, and no more. And if you spend less than the amount, you will discipline yourself to put the difference you did not spend in a cookie jar or a piggy bank when you get home. Then you actually did 2 things. You spent less than you thought you would and by saving the difference you did not spend you created a savings account as well. In addition, when you get your statement and pay the entire amount you will then be left with a zero balance. Therefore you DO NOT incur any interest expense, you are simply paying for the goods you bought at the price you paid, NOT A PENNY MORE. You are actually using their money, in effect actually borrowing the money for a short period interest free. This type of action creates a pattern of good behavior that ultimately generates an excellent credit report necessary in the future.

If we go back into the history of the credit card, you will find they were originally called charge cards not credit cards, simply because the amount charged was paid in full when the bill came, no credit beyond the amount spent was extended. The inventor of the first bank issued card was John Biggins, in 1946, of the Flatbush National Bank in Brooklyn, N.Y. He created a program between bank customers and local merchants, called "Charge-It Merchants deposited sales slips into the bank and the bank billed the customer who used the card. In 1950, the Diners Club issued a credit card, invented by Diners Club founder Frank McNamara. It was intended solely to pay restaurant bills. A customer could eat at a restaurant without cash that accepted the Diners Club card. Diners Club would pay the restaurant and the customer repaid Diners Club. Again, it was a charge card since it was expecting the entire bill to be paid in full when received by the customer. American Express issued their first credit card in 1958. Bank of America also issued their first card in 1958 called BankAmericard [now Visa]. Credit cards were first promoted by traveling salesman common in that era for use on the road. It was a convenience, a time saving device rather than a form of credit.

Life is always about choices. We're faced with them constantly on a daily basis. Temptations are there it's up to us to decide whether we take the bait or resist. Disciplines are necessary for a healthy body, a healthy mind and financial health as well. Receiving credit cards is a temptation. No one forces you to use them. Lets have more self control, and ask yourself the simple question I mentioned earlier. One credit card is all you need. Your ability to pay back what you spend is different for everyone. Don't spend what you cannot pay back in its entirety when that statement arrives. We are a society of consumers and the credit card companies know it. We always think buy now pay later. We're programmed to think that way after many years of brain washing from advertisers to think that way.

It's the complete opposite of the generations of the 40s, 50s and even the 60s. They still believed in paying for things in full in cash. Credit cards the way we know them today didn't exist. One could argue credit is important to grow an economy. Very true however as usually what starts out as a simple concept gets out of hand. When credit cards began in department stores they were specific product centric. In other words a specific need was being filled and paid off over a specific period of time. A refrigerator, washing machine etc. They were NEED BASED. As they expanded into general products people used them like cash and became less sensitized to spending, buying became WANT BASED. You go into a store see something you want. buy it, I'll pay for it later. When you use cash its different. If you go into a store and something costs $500 and you only have $300 you have to get more cash or walk out of the store. Even if you have the $500 and count it out and pay for it. You realize you're a lot lighter in the pocket or pocket book and you didn't come home with something else you didn't set out to buy. If you saw something else you wanted and you did not have anymore cash you had to pass on it. Its, physical, its real, it happened. Credit cards disconnected the customer from the physical cash, the process became surriel and the buyers remorse only comes when the statement arrives and by then it was too late.

So, what do you do to get out from under if in fact you get caught in the trap. Lets assume you start using your card and for what ever reason you start running up a balance. Bad things sometimes happen to good people. Life throws you a curve ball, the credit card is a way out and things get out of control. You now have to adapt to the problem, adjust your way of spending and overcome the problem. When you get the bill, check the dollar amount of interest you are being charged. Then check the "minimum payment"due. The payment you make must cover the entire interest dollar amount they are charging you plus twice that amount to reduce your principal owed. Lets look at an example. You get a credit card bill that you owe $1000. The minimum payment they want you to pay is $15.00 and the interest charged is $17.50. Clearly if you do the math and pay the minimum payment only you will never reduce the amount you owe. So, using my method mentioned above you would pay $17.50 [interest being charged] PLUS $35.00 [two times $17.50] or a payment of $52.50. Obviously you should pay the entire balance as soon as you can, my method is the minimum approach to attack the balance. Another suggestion is to reach out to the credit card company and ask them to reduce the interest rate they are charging you. Many times they will accommodate you if you have been paying your bills on time. Remember it's a business they want to keep you. After all they don't want to lose a customer that pays their bills. So, always pay on time even if you only can pay the minimum. Then when you call them and ask them to lower your rate they will be more likely to work with you, Lastly check zero interest card promotions that want to do balance transfers. You may be able to move your balance from a high interest rate to another card with a zero rate. Be aware of the time period that it will be zero and what the rate will be after the promotional period. If done carefully it can help quite a bit. Run your household as if it were a business. First, take care of your needs before you go after your wants. When you have discretionary income save it before you spend it. Lastly, keep a reserve for the unexpected expenses that inevitably occur to all of us.

Remember, timing is not the answer; time is. Lost opportunity is always better than lost capital. No one can predict the markets accurately, regardless of how much technology or education the person has. But your needs can be predicted, and combined with the commonsense approach, your needs can be accommodated. Will Rogers said it best:

"The return of my money is much more important than the so-called return on my money."

So stop waiting for the perfect investment. Forget about stock tips. Listen to music, not to market forecasters, and take control. There is no time like the present, go for it!

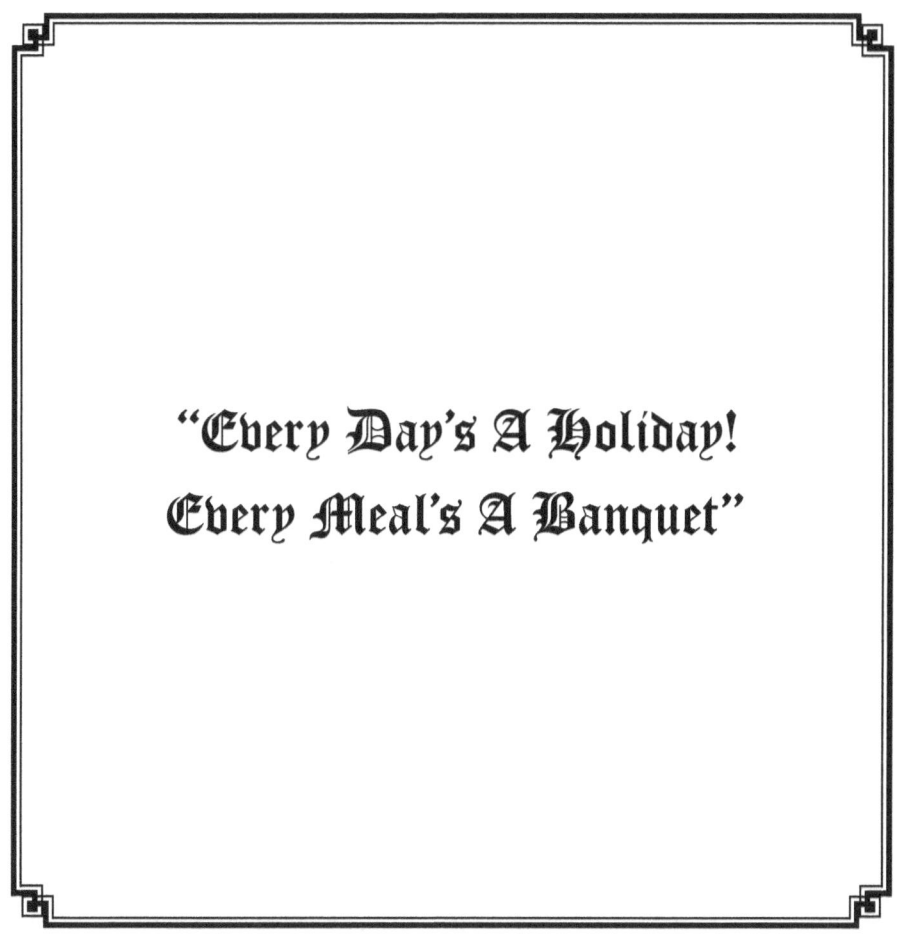

Summary

The following list summarizes the main points that were presented in this book. If you keep these points in mind, reaching your financial goals should be an easy task.

1. Pay yourself first (401-k account, IRA account, money market account, etc.).

2. Don't speculate—invest!

3. Empower yourself, don't depend on others.

4. Choose uncomplicated solutions to everyday financial problems.

5. Remember that investing is a journey in which direction is more important than speed.

6. Balance your financial diet.

7. Prudence, intellect, perception—you have them, so use them.

8. Age equals percent of fixed income.

9. Don't mistake gambling for investing.

10. Prepare, don't predict.

11. Bonds are the key ingredients.

12. Exercise discipline and diligence—if you're lazy, you'll lose.

13. High-yield bonds are called junk bonds for a reason.

14. Start saving and investing as early as you can and as often as you can.

15. Get children involved early.

16. Sugar highs have no nutritional value.

17. Use credit cards wisely—for needs not wants—charge only what you can pay back in full when the bill comes

18. CDs can be bought at brokerage firms also

19. Ladder maturities when purchasing bonds

20. If you want to buy a mutual fund or bond fund read about fees and other details carefully.

Glossary

BASIS POINT One basis point is equal to one one-hundredth of a percent of the yield (1/100th of 1 percent).

BOND RATING A system of evaluating the credit quality of a company's bonds. The bonds are assigned letter ratings based on various risk classifications. Aaa is the highest investment grade, and Baa (Moody's) and BBB (Standard and Poors) are the lowest of the investment-grade categories.

CALL Some bonds have call features. The issuer has the ability to call or redeem (retire) the bond on a specific date or at varying specified intervals. A bond that is noncallable is designated N.C.

CALLABLE also referred to as redeemable is feature on a bond or CD that may be called or redeemed by the issuer prior to maturity at a specific predetermined price fully disclosed when the bond or CD was issued. In most cases the price is $1000 [also referred to as PAR], The call price can be a price other that $1000. Check before buying a callable bond or CD what that call feature and price are before purchasing.

COUPON RATE The annual rate of interest the issuer promises to pay the bondholder.

CURRENT YIELD The interest payment divided by the dollar price equals the current yield. A 7 percent coupon on a bond trading at 99 ($990) equals 7.07 percent. The yield to maturity and the current yield can differ.

DIAMONDS [DIA} trust series 1 ETF follows the performance of the Dow Jones Industrial Average Index or DJII a.k.a. the Dow. There is a direct correlation between the DJIA and DIA, therefore it allows an investor to get exposure to the Dow without having to buy all 30 stocks individually. It trades under the symbol DIA.

ESTATE PUT FEATURE, SURVIVORS PUT OPTION, DEATH PUT all three phrases refer to a feature that some certificates of deposits { CDs} have that are issued by brokerage firms. They allow the estate of a deceased individual that owned a CD to redeem that CD at par [$1000] regardless of market price.

ETF Exchange Traded Fund—this is a security that tracks an index or basket of assets and trades like a stock on an exchange throughout the day when shares are bought and sold. Since it trades like a stock, its value is determine by buyers and sellers during the trading day. A mutual funds value is determined solely by its 'net asset value' {NAV} at the end of the day.

FIXED-INCOME SECURITY A bond or preferred stock with a stated percentage or dollar income return.

GOVERNMENT BOND An IOU from the U.S. Treasury, considered the safest of investments; U.S. Treasury issues are available in a wide variety of maturities.

MATURITY The date that the principal amount or stated amount of the bond comes due and is payable to the bondholder.

NASDAQ 100 trade under the symbol QQQ. This is an ETF that tracks the Nasdaq 100 stock index

NON-CALL is a feature that a bond or CD have. It means that they cannot be called or redeemed prior to maturity. Also referred to as a "bullet"

PAR Usually referred to as the principal amount of a bond; quoted in numerical fashion as 100, meaning $1,000 per bond.

POINT One point in dollars when referring to stocks is $1.00. When referring to bonds, one point is $10. Bonds are quoted as a percentage of $1,000 par value amounts. A stock quoted 90-91 means $90-$91. A bond quoted 90-91 means $900-$910.

QUOTE The bid and offer prices of a security. The bid is the price that a market maker is willing to pay for a security (the price at which you can sell it), and an offer price is the price that a market maker is willing to sell a security (where you can buy it).

RULE OF 72 A simple formula that can approximate the amount of time it will take for money to double at a given compound interest rate. Simply divide 72 by the interest rate. For instance, a 7 percent bond would take 10.2 years to double in value (72 ÷ 7 = 10.2 yrs). An 8 percent bond would mature in 9 years, a 6 percent bond would double in 12 years, and so on.

STANDARD & POORS 500, S&P 500 [Spiders, Spyders, SPDR} trade under the symbol SPY. SPY is an ETF designed to track the S&P 500 index.

YIELD Income received from an investment, usually referred to as a percentage.

YIELD TO MATURITY Rate of return held on a debt security held to maturity. Interest payments, capital gain or loss, and reinvestment of coupon all are taken into account.

ZERO COUPON BOND A bond that does not make periodic interest payments but instead is issued at a deep discount from its face value.

Dow Jones Industrial Average

Companies are added and deleted periodically

From Wikipedia, the free encyclopedia

The **Dow Jones Industrial Average,** also called the **Industrial Average,** the **Dow Jones,** the **Dow Jones Industrial,** the **Dow 30**, or simply the **Dow,** is a stock market index, and one of several indices created by *Wall Street Journal* editor and Dow Jones & Company co-founder Charles Dow. The industrial average was first calculated on

May 26, 1896.[1] Currently owned by S&P Dow Jones Indices, which is majority owned by McGraw-Hill Financial, it is the most notable of the Dow Averages, of which the first (non-industrial) was first published on February 16, 1885. The averages are named after Dow and one of his business associates, statistician Edward Jones. It is an index that shows how 30 large publicly owned companies based in the United States have traded during a standard trading session in the stock market.[3] It is the second oldest U.S. market index after the Dow Jones Transportation Average, which was also created by Dow.

The *Industrial* portion of the name is largely historical, as many of the modern 30 components have little or nothing to do with traditional heavy industry. The average is price-weighted, and to compensate for the effects of stock splits and other adjustments, it is currently a scaled average. The value of the Dow is not the actual average of the prices of its component stocks, but rather the sum of the component prices divided by a divisor, which changes whenever one of the component stocks has a stock split or stock dividend, so as to generate a consistent value for the index. Since the divisor is currently less than one, the value of the index is larger than the sum of the component prices.

Components

Beginning on September 23, 2013, the Dow Jones Industrial Average will consist of the following 30 major American companies:

1. 3M
2. American Express
3. AT&T
4. Boeing
5. Caterpillar
6. Chevron Corporation
7. Cisco Systems
8. Coca-Cola
9. DuPont
10. ExxonMobil
11. General Electric
12. Goldman Sachs
13. The Home Depot
14. Intel
15. IBM
16. Johnson & Johnson
17. JPMorgan Chase
18. McDonald's
19. Merck
20. Microsoft
21. Nike
22. Pfizer
23. Procter & Gamble
24. Travelers
25. UnitedHealth Group
26. United Technologies Corporation
27. Verizon
28. Visa
29. Wal-Mart
30. Walt Disney

NASDAQ-100

Companies are added and deleted periodically

From Wikipedia, the free encyclopedia

The **NASDAQ-100** is a stock market index of 100 of the largest non-financial companies listed on the NASDAQ. It is a modified capitalization-weighted index. The companies' weights in the index are based on their market capitalizations, with certain rules capping the influence of the largest components. It does not contain financial companies, and includes companies incorporated outside the United States. Both of those factors differentiate it from the Dow Jones Industrial Average, and the exclusion of financial companies distinguishes it from the S&P 500.

Components

This list is current as prior to the market open on September 9, 2013. An up-to-date list is available in the External Links section. It should be noted that this is an alphabetical list, and not a ranked list

1. 21st Century Fox (FOXA)

2. Activision Blizzard (ATVI)

3. Adobe Systems Incorporated (ADBE)

4. Akamai Technologies, Inc (AKAM)

5. Alexion Pharmaceuticals (ALXN)

6. Altera Corporation (ALTR)

7. Amazon.com, Inc. (AMZN)

8. Amgen Inc. (AMGN)

9. Analog Devices (ADI)

10. Apple Inc. (AAPL)

11. Applied Materials, Inc. (AMAT)

12. Autodesk, Inc. (ADSK)

13. Automatic Data Processing, Inc. (ADP)

14. Avago Technologies, Inc. (AVGO)

15. Baidu.com, Inc. (BIDU)

16. Bed Bath & Beyond Inc. (BBBY)

17. Biogen Idec, Inc (BIIB)

18. Broadcom Corporation (BRCM)

19. C. H. Robinson Worldwide, Inc. (CHRW)

20. CA, Inc. (CA)

21. Catamaran Corporation (CTRX)

22. Celgene Corporation (CELG)

23. Cerner Corporation (CERN)

24. Charter Communications, Inc. (CHTR)

25. Check Point Software Technologies Ltd. (CHKP)

26. Cisco Systems, Inc. (CSCO)

27. Citrix Systems, Inc. (CTXS)

28. Cognizant Technology Solutions Corporation (CTSH)

29. Comcast Corporation (CMCSA)

30. Costco Wholesale Corporation (COST)

31. Dell Inc. (DELL)

32. DENTSPLY International Inc. (XRAY)

33. DirecTV (DTV)

34. Discovery Communications (DISCA)

35. Dollar Tree, Inc. (DLTR)

36. eBay Inc. (EBAY)

37. Equinix (EQIX)

38. Expedia, Inc. (EXPE)

39. Expeditors International of Washington, Inc. (EXPD)

40. Express Scripts, Inc. (ESRX)

41. F5 Networks, Inc. (FFIV)

42. Facebook, Inc. (FB)

43. Fastenal Company (FAST)

44. Fiserv, Inc. (FISV)

45. Fossil, Inc. (FOSL)

46. Garmin Ltd. (GRMN)

47. Gilead Sciences, Inc. (GILD)

48. Google Inc. (GOOG)

49. Green Mountain Coffee Roasters (GMCR)

50. Henry Schein, Inc. (HSIC)

51. Intel Corporation (INTC)

52. Intuit, Inc. (INTU)

53. Intuitive Surgical Inc. (ISRG)

54. KLA Tencor Corporation (KLAC)

55. Kraft Foods (KRFT)

56. Liberty Global (LBTYA)

57. Liberty Interactive (LINTA)

58. Liberty Media (LMCA)

59. Linear Technology Corporation (LLTC)

60. Mattel, Inc. (MAT)

61. Maxim Integrated Products (MXIM)

62. Microchip Technology Incorporated (MCHP)

63. Micron Technology, Inc. (MU)

64. Microsoft Corporation (MSFT)

65. Mondelēz International (MDLZ)

66. Monster Beverage (MNST)

67. Mylan, Inc. (MYL)

68. NetApp, Inc. (NTAP)

69. Netflix (NFLX)

70. Nuance Communications, Inc. (NUAN)

71. NVIDIA Corporation (NVDA)

72. O'Reilly Automotive, Inc. (ORLY)

73. PACCAR Inc. (PCAR)

74. Paychex, Inc. (PAYX)

75. Priceline.com, Incorporated (PCLN)

76. QUALCOMM Incorporated (QCOM)

77. Randgold Resources, Ltd. (GOLD)

78. Regeneron Pharmaceuticals (REGN)

79. Ross Stores Inc. (ROST)

80. SanDisk Corporation (SNDK)

81. SBA Communications (SBAC)

82. Seagate Technology Holdings (STX)

83. Sears Holdings Corporation (SHLD)

84. Sigma-Aldrich Corporation (SIAL)

85. Sirius XM Radio, Inc. (SIRI)

86. Staples Inc. (SPLS)

87. Starbucks Corporation (SBUX)

88. Stericycle, Inc (SRCL)

89. Symantec Corporation (SYMC)

90. Texas Instruments, Inc. (TXN)

91. Tesla Motors, Inc. (TSLA)

92. Verisk Analytics (VRSK)

93. Vertex Pharmaceuticals (VRTX)

94. Viacom Inc. (VIAB)

95. Vodafone Group, plc. (VOD)

96. Western Digital (WDC)

97. Whole Foods Market, Inc. (WFM)

98. Wynn Resorts Ltd. (WYNN)

99. Xilinx, Inc. (XLNX)

100. Yahoo! Inc. (YHOO)

List of S&P 500 companies

Companies are added and deleted periodically

From Wikipedia, the free encyclopedia

The **S&P 500** stock market index, maintained by S&P Dow Jones Indices, comprises 500 large-cap American companies covering about 75 percent of the American equity market by capitalization. The index is weighted by market capitalization, so large companies account for relatively more of the index. The index constituents and the constituent weights are updated regularly using rules published by S&P Dow Jones Indices. The index constituents listed below were current as of the start of the trading day of June 7, 2013.

S&P 500 Companies

Standard and Poor's has created an index of 500 top publicly-traded companies. The companies cover a broad array of industries. This index is often used as a comparison for performance of stocks and mutual funds.

3M Company
Abbott Labs
Abercrombie and Fitch
Adobe Systems
Advanced Micro Devices
AES Corp.
Aetna Inc.
Affiliated Computer
AFLAC Inc.
Agilent Technologies
Air Products & Chemicals
AK Steel Holding
Akamai
Alcoa Inc
Allegheny Energy
Allegheny Technologies Inc
Allergan, Inc.
Allstate Corp.
Altera Corp.
Altria Group, Inc.
Amazon.com

Amerada Hess
Ameren Corporation
American Capital
American Electric Power
American Express
American Int'l. Group
American Power Conversion
American Standard
American Tower
Ameriprise Financial
AmerisourceBergen Corp.
Amgen
Amphenol
Anadarko Petroleum
Analog Devices
Anheuser-Busch
Aon Corp.
Apache Corp.

Apartment Investment & Mgmt'
Apollo Group
Apple Computer
Applera Corp
Applied Materials
Archer-Daniels-Midland
Archstone-Smith Trust
Ashland Inc.
Assurant
AT&T Corp.
Autodesk, Inc.
Automatic Data Processing Inc.
AutoNation, Inc.
AutoZone Inc.
Avalon Bay Communities
Avery Dennison Corp.
Avon Products
Baker Hughes
Ball Corp.

The Investor's Survival Guide

Bank of America Corp.
Bank of New York Mellon
Bard (C.R.) Inc.
Barr Pharmaceuticals
Baxter International Inc.
BB&T Corporation
Becton, Dickinson
Bed Bath & Beyond
Bemis Company
Best Buy
Big Lots, Inc.
BIOGEN IDEC Inc.
BJ Services
Black & Decker Corp.
Block H&R
BMC Software
Boeing Company
Boston Properties
Boston Scientific
Bristol-Myers Squibb
Broadcom Corporation
Brown-Forman Corp.
Burlington Northern Santa Fe
Cablevision
Cabot Oil and Gas
Cameron International
Campbell Soup
Capital One Financial
Cardinal Health, Inc.
Carnival Corp.
Caterpillar Inc.
CBS
CenterPoint Energy
Century Telephone
Cephalon
CF Industries
Charles Schwab
Chevron Corp.
Chubb Corp.
Ciena Corp.
CIGNA Corp.
Cincinnati Financial
Cintas Corporation
Cisco Systems
Citigroup Inc.
Citizens Communications
Citrix Systems
Clorox Co.
CMS Energy
Coach, Inc.
Coca Cola Co.
Coca-Cola Enterprises
Colgate-Palmolive
Comcast Corp.
Comerica Inc.
Compass Bancshares
Computer Associates Intl.
Computer Sciences Corp.
Compuware Corp.
Comverse Technology
ConAgra Foods
ConocoPhillips
Consolidated Edison
CONSOL Energy
Constellation Brands
Constellation Energy Group
Convergys Corp.
Cooper Industries, Ltd.
Corning
Costco
Coventry Healthcare
CSX Corp.
Cummins Inc.
CVS Caremark.
Dana Corp.
Danaher Corp.
Darden Restaurants
Davita

89

Dean Foods
Deere & Co.
Dell Inc.
Denbury Resources
Dentsply International
Devon Energy Corp.
Devry
Discover Financial
Dollar General
Dominion Resources
Donnelley (R.R.) & Sons
Dover Corp.
Dow Chemical
D.R. Horton
Dr. Pepper Snapple Group
DTE Energy Co.
Du Pont (E.I.)
Duke Energy
Dun and Bradstreet
Dynegy
E*Trade Financial Corp.
Eastman Chemical
Eastman Kodak
Eaton Corp.
eBay Inc.
Ecolab Inc.
Edison Int'l
El Paso Corp.

Electronic Arts
Electronic Data Systems
Embarq
EMC Corp.
Emerson Electric
Entergy Corp.
EOG Resources
Estee Lauder
Equifax Inc.
Equity Office Properties
Equity Residential
Exelon Corp.
Express Scripts
Exxon Mobil Corp.
Family Dollar Stores
Fannie Mae
Federal Home Loan Mtg.
Federated Dept. Stores
Federated Investors Inc.
FedEx Corporation
Fifth Third Bancorp
First Data
First Horizon National
FirstEnergy Corp.
Flserv Inc.
Fisher Scientific

Fluor Corp. (New)
Ford Motor
Forest Laboratories
Fortune Brands, Inc.
FPL Group
Franklin Resources
Freeport-McMoran Cp & Gld
Freescale Semiconductor Inc.
Gannett Co.
Gap
General Dynamics
General Electric
General Mills
General Motors
Genuine Parts
Genworth Financial
Genzyme Corp.
Gilead Sciences
Golden West Financial
Goldman Sachs Group
Goodrich Corporation
Goodyear Tire & Rubber
Google
Grainger (W.W.) Inc.
Great Lakes Chemical

The Investor's Survival Guide

Halliburton Co.
Harley-Davidson
Harman International
Harrah's Entertainment
Hartford Financial Svc. Gp.
Hasbro Inc.
HCA Inc.
Health Management Assoc.
Heinz (H.J.)
Hercules, Inc.
Hewlett-Packard
Hilton Hotels
Home Depot
Honeywell Int'l Inc.
Hospira Inc.
Humana Inc.
Huntington Bancshares
Illinois Tool Works
IMS Health Inc.
Ingersoll-Rand Co. Ltd.
Intel Corp.
International Bus. Machines
International Flav/Frag
International Game Technology
International Paper

Interpublic Group
Intuit, Inc.
ITT Industries, Inc.
Jabil Circuit
Janus Capital Group
JDS Uniphase Corp
Johnson & Johnson
Johnson Controls
Jones Apparel Group
JPMorgan Chase & Co.
Juniper Networks
KB Home
Kellogg Co.
Kerr-McGee
KeyCorp
Keyspan Energy
Kimberly-Clark
Kinder Morgan
King Pharmaceuticals
Kimco Realty
KLA-Tencor Corp.
Kohl's Corp.
Kroger Co.
L-3 Communications Holdings
Laboratory Corp. of America Holding
Leggett & Platt
Legg Mason
Lehman Bros.

Lennar
Lexmark Int'l
Lilly (Eli) & Co.
Limited Brands, Inc.
Lincoln National
Linear Technology Corp.
Liz Claiborne, Inc.
Lockheed Martin Corp.
Loews Corp.
Louisiana Pacific
Lowe's Cos.
LSI Logic
Lucent Technologies
M&T Bank Corp.
Manitowoc
Marathon Oil Corp.
Marriott Int'l.
Marsh & McLennan
Marshall & Ilsley Corp.
Masco Corp.
Massey Energy
MasterCard
Mattel, Inc.
Maxim Integrated Prod
Maytag Corp.
MBIA Inc.
McCormick & Co.

McDonald's Corp.
McGraw-Hill
McKesson Corp.
MeadWestvaco Corporation
Medco Health Solutions Inc.
MedImmune Inc.
Medtronic Inc.
Merck & Co.
Meredith Corp.
MetLife Inc.
Metro PCS
MGIC Investment
Micron Technology
Microsoft Corp.
Millipore Corp.
Molex Inc.
Molson Coors Brewing Company
Monsanto Co.
Monster Worldwide
Moody's Corp
Morgan Stanley
Motorola Inc.
Murphy Oil
Mylan Laboratories
Nabors Industries Ltd.
Nasdaq OMX Group
National Oilwell Varco, Inc.
National Semiconductor
Navistar International
Netflix
Network Appliance
Newell Rubbermaid Co.
Newfield Exploration
Newmont Mining Corp.
News Corporation
NICOR Inc.
NIKE Inc.
NiSource Inc.
Nordstrom
Norfolk Southern Corp.
Northeast Utilities
Northern Trust Corp.
Northrop Grumman Corp.
Novell Inc.
Novellus Systems
Nucor Corp.
NVIDIA Corp.
NYSE Euronext
Occidental Petroleum
Omnicom Group
Oracle Corp.
O'Reilly Automotive
Owens-Illinois
PACCAR Inc.
Pactiv Corp.
Pall Corp.
Parametric Technology
Parker-Hannifin
Patterson Cos.
Paychex Inc.
Penney (J.C.)
Peoples Energy
Pepsi Bottling Group
PepsiCo Inc.
PerkinElmer
Pfizer, Inc.
PG&E Corp.
Phelps Dodge
Pinnacle West Capital
Pitney-Bowes
Plum Creek Timber Co.
PMC-Sierra Inc.
PNC Bank Corp.
PPG Industries
PPL Corp.
Praxair, Inc.
Principal Financial Group
Procter & Gamble

Progress Energy, Inc.
Progressive Corp.
ProLogis
Prudential Financial
Public Serv. Enterprise Inc.
Public Storage
Pulte Homes, Inc.
QLogic Corp.
QUALCOMM Inc.
Quest Diagnostics
Qwest Communications Int
RadioShack Corp
Raytheon Co.
Realogy
Reebok International
Regions Financial Corp. (New)
Reynolds American Inc.
Robert Half International
Rockwell Automation, Inc.
Rockwell Collins
Rohm & Haas
Rowan Cos.
Ryder System
Sabre Holding Corp.

SAFECO Corp.
Safeway Inc.
Sandisk
Sanmina-SCI Corp.
Sara Lee Corp.
Schering-Plough
Schlumberger Ltd.
Scripps (E.W.)
Sealed Air Corp.
Sears Holdings Corporation
Sempra Energy
Sherwin-Williams
Sigma-Aldrich
Simon Property Group, Inc
SLM Corporation
Snap-On Inc.
Solectron
Southern Co.
Southwest Airlines
Sovereign Bancorp
Sprint Corp. FON
St Jude Medical
St. Paul Travelers Cos.
Stanley Works
Staples Inc.
Starbucks Corp.
Starwood Hotels & Resorts
State Street Corp.
Stryker Corp.
Sun Microsystems

Sunoco, Inc.
SunTrust Banks
Supervalu Inc.
Symantec Corp.
Symbol Technologies
Synovus Financial
Sysco Corp.
T. Rowe Price Group
Target Corp.
TECO Energy
Tektronix Inc.
Tellabs, Inc.
Temple-Inland
Tenet Healthcare Corp.
Teradyne Inc.
Texas Instruments
Textron Inc.
The Hershey Company
Thermo Electron
Tiffany & Co.
Time Warner Inc.
TJX Companies Inc.
Torchmark Corp.
Toys R Us, Inc.
Transocean Inc.
Tribune Co.
TXU Corp.
Tyson Foods
Tyco International

U.S. Bancorp
Union Pacific
Unisys Corp.
United Health Group Inc.
United Parcel Service
United States Steel Corp.
United Technologies
Univision Communications
UnumProvident Corp.
UST Inc.
V.F. Corp.
Valero Energy
Verizon Communications
Viacom Inc.
Vornado Realty Trust
Vulcan Materials
Wachovia Corp.
Wal-Mart Stores
Walgreen Co.
Walt Disney Co.
Washington Mutual
Waste Management Inc.
Waters Corporation
Watson Pharmaceuticals

Weatherford International
WellPoint Inc.
Wells Fargo
Wendy's International
Weyerhaeuser Corp.
Whirlpool Corp.
Windstream
Whole Foods Market
Williams Cos.
Wrigley (Wm) Jr.
Wyeth
Wyndham Worldwide
Xcel Energy Inc
Xerox Corp.
Xilinx, Inc
XL Capital
XTO Energy Inc.
Yahoo Inc.
Yum! Brands, Inc
Zimmer Holdings
Zions Bancorp

www.ingramcontent.com/pod-product-compliance
Lightning Source LLC
Chambersburg PA
CBHW030859180526
45163CB00004B/1635